Modern Cars

Contents	Page

written by Suzette Toms

It starts with design

Car design has changed over the years as designers have adopted new tools and experimented with ways to think of new products. For most car designers today, computers have the tools they use to draw concepts and designs.

2

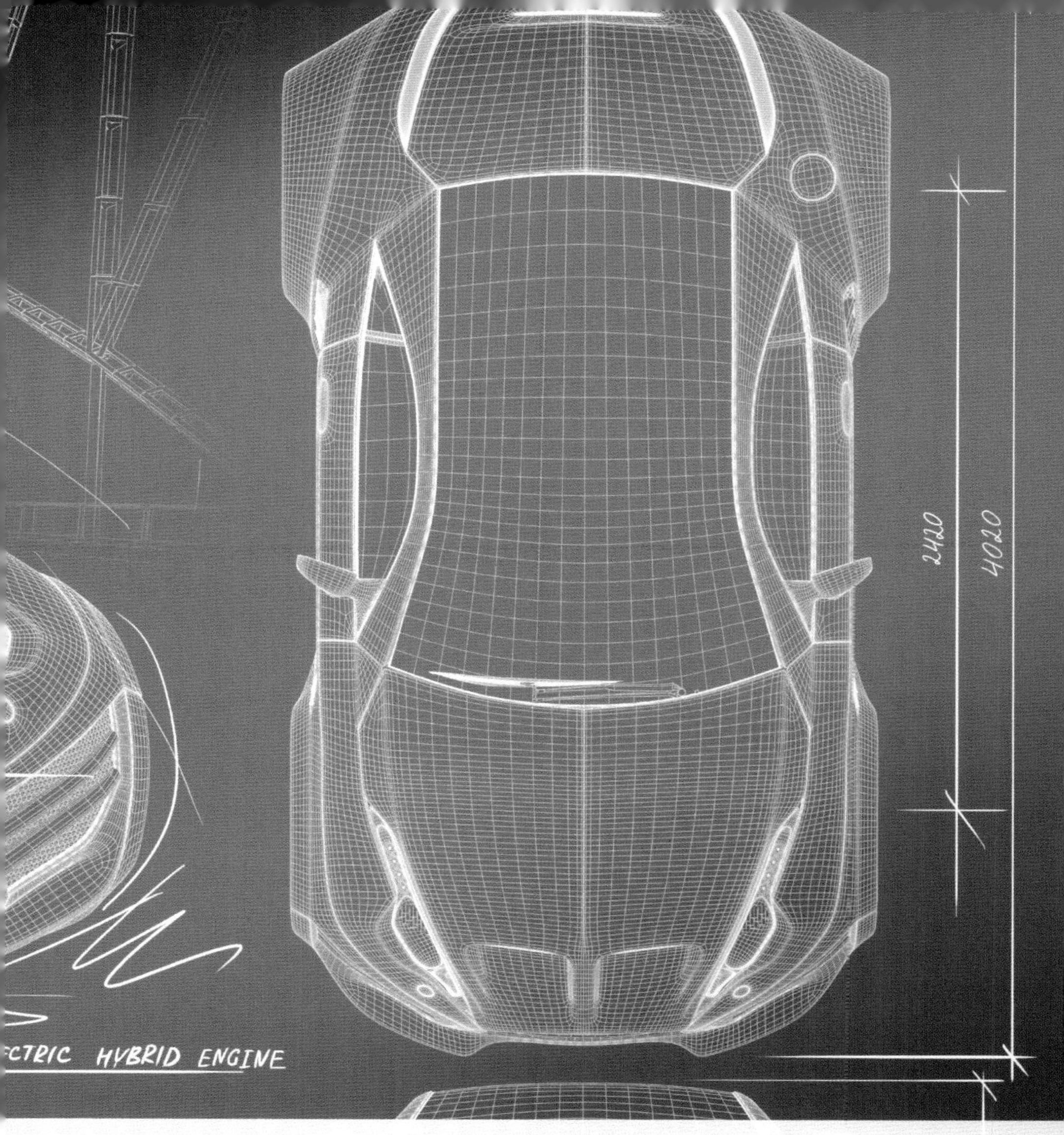

Almost every new car design begins with a simple sketch. Creating this "concept art" needs lots of research. For ideas, designers look at present cars, past cars, different materials, fashion trends, and they might also use images from nature.

3D models

Models can be made from a variety of materials, including wood, foam and plastic. Today there are also computer programs that turn concept sketches into three-dimensional images (3D) to show what the vehicle will look like from different angles. All models are tested to find out what changes might be needed: e.g. tests using virtual wind tunnels help designers find the most aerodynamic shapes.

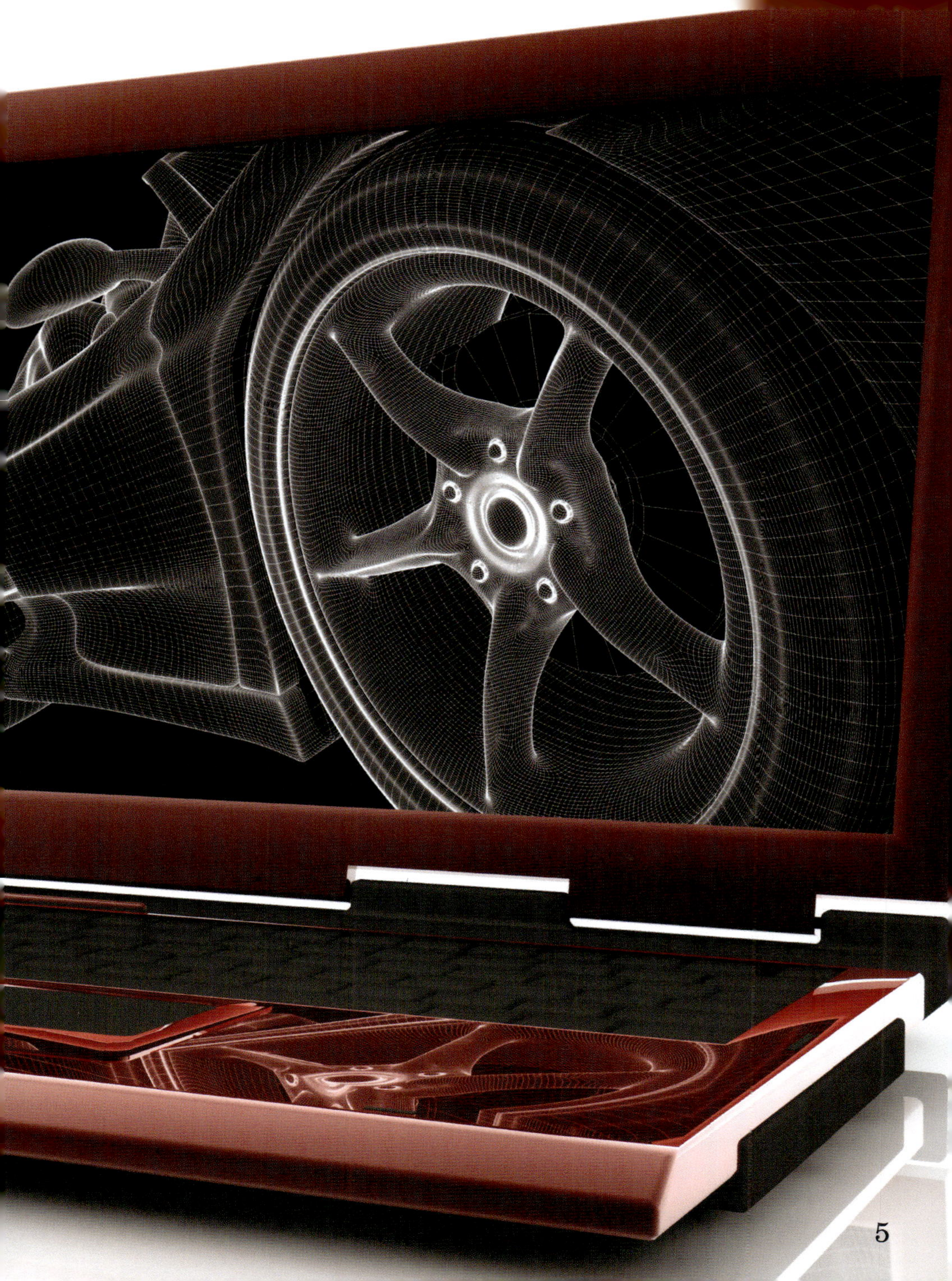

Concept cars

Concept cars are full-scale models used to test the designs. Some concept cars are just plastic bodies with no engine parts, while others are real working vehicles used to test and show their systems and performance. These concept cars are also used to measure public interest in a new model before a company decides to spend money to produce it.

Testing

All manufacturers must make sure
that their vehicles meet government
safety standards and stand up to
normal driver use. One of the most
well-known tests is crash testing,
where dummies are put inside the
car to act as "passengers". These
crash tests are held to show what
happens to passengers in cars that
crash at different speeds.
The car manufacturers need to
check that their vehicles meet lots
of quality and safety measurements.
They measure these things:

* safety
* noise
* vibration
* comfort
* fuel efficiency
* fuel emissions
* performance under extreme
  conditions.

Production plants

All the parts for today's cars are made by specialist manufacturers
from all around the world and sent to many different production
plants. These are factories where vehicle parts are put together
by skilled workers and robotic systems to make the final product –
a car.

Chassis

The chassis is the base of the car. It is a welded frame to which all other parts of the car are attached. The first parts attached are called "running gear". This includes the engine, front and rear suspension, fuel tank, rear-end and half-shafts, transmission, drive shaft, gear box, steering box, wheel drums and the brake systems. Robots and skilled workers are given different tasks, with robots attaching the heavier pieces. Power tools are used to bolt each part into place.

Body

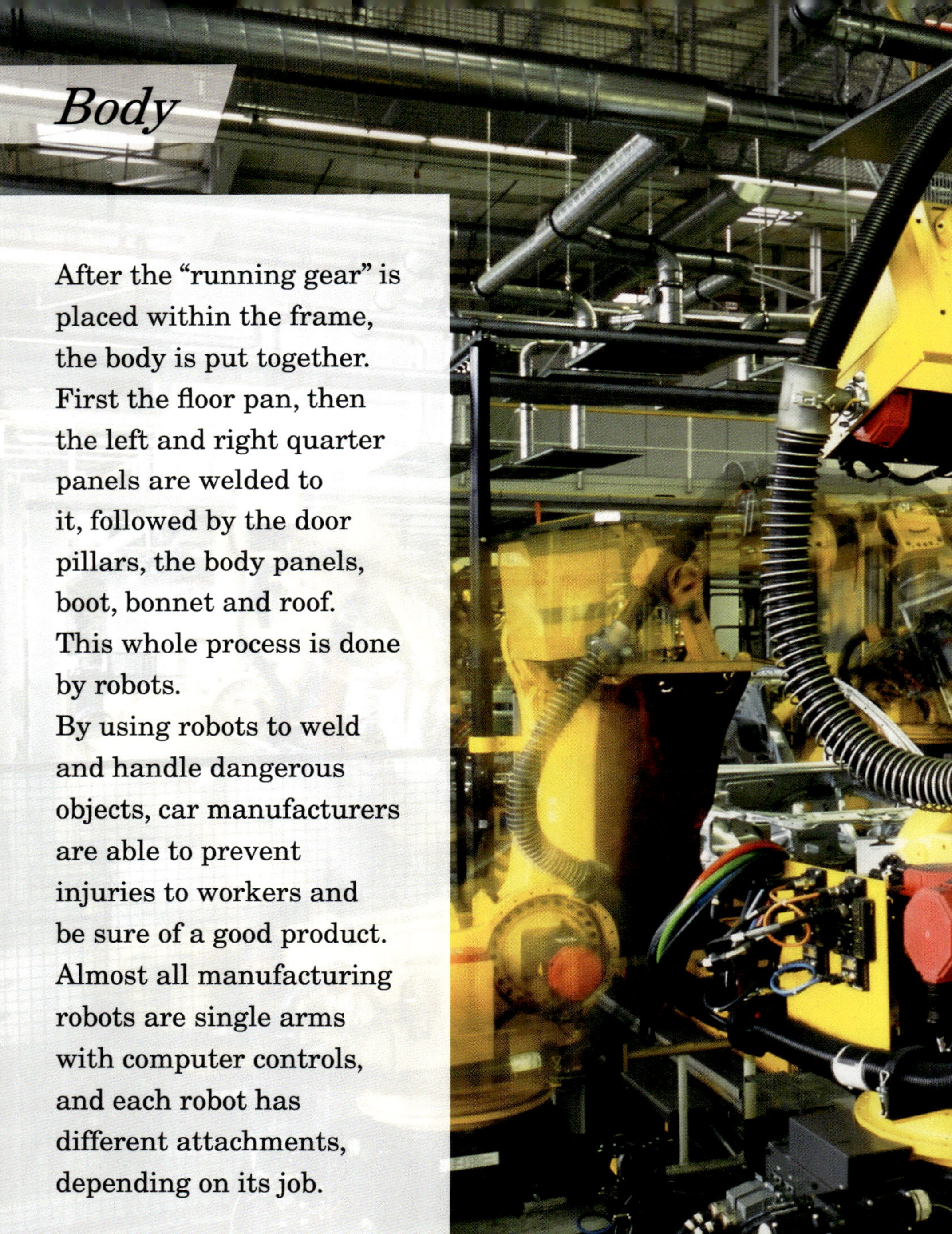

After the "running gear" is placed within the frame, the body is put together. First the floor pan, then the left and right quarter panels are welded to it, followed by the door pillars, the body panels, boot, bonnet and roof. This whole process is done by robots.

By using robots to weld and handle dangerous objects, car manufacturers are able to prevent injuries to workers and be sure of a good product. Almost all manufacturing robots are single arms with computer controls, and each robot has different attachments, depending on its job.

Paint

Before a car is painted, skilled workers check it for dents or faults. When it has passed this test, the car is "dipped" with primer to clean it, and then oven-dried ready to be painted. After this, the body is given a special bath to apply the undercoat paint, which allows the final coats of paint to stick to it. Paint is sprayed on by robotic painters and then finished with high heat treatment.

Interior

Next the interior parts are added. These are: instruments, wiring, dashboard, inside lights, seats, door trims and panels, stereos, speakers, glass, steering wheel, weather strips, brakes, pedals and carpets.

The chassis and body are put together before the wheels, battery, fuel and final trim are added. This work is done by robots to make sure there is a perfect fit between the body and the chassis, all finished in the fastest time.

Final inspection

Before a car can be sent to a dealer for sale, a final inspection is made on the engine. The body is also given a water test to make sure that the doors, bonnet and boot lid fit properly. Finally the vehicle is ready to be driven off the production line for a wheel check and a test drive. The average car takes only about 12 hours to build! The number of cars produced each hour depends on the size of the production line.

Future production

As the cost grows for the fossil fuels that cars use now, there is a need for new and different fuels. Governments and car manufacturers are working on the development of environment-friendly vehicles to find an answer to this problem. The electric car is already here, and there are cars being built that are powered by the sun or the wind!

In the future the look, function and design of our cars is sure to change with the result of new technology, research and experiments.